Erasing My Sanity!

BY KIMBERLY CHAMBERS

Published by Great Quotations Publishing Co.,
8102 Lemont Road, #300
Woodridge, IL 60517

Library of Congress Catalog Number: 98-71847

ISBN 1-56245-346-7

Printed in Hong Kong 2004

DEDICATION:

TO MY MOTHER AND FATHER, AND TO MY HUSBAND, ROBERT.

STRESS IS:
KNOWING YOUR WORST
PICTURE IS IN HUNDREDS
OF SCHOOL YEARBOOKS.

YOU'RE CALLED OUT OF CLASS TO TAKE AN IMPORTANT PHONE CALL—FROM A TELEPHONE SOLICITOR.

STRESS IS:
LEAVING THE
CLASS PET AT SCHOOL
OVER SPRING BREAK.

YOU'RE STUCK IN TRAFFIC WHEN YOU SHOULD BE IN A MEETING WITH YOUR NEW PRINCIPAL.

Aa Bb Cc Dd Ee Ff Gg Hh Ii Jj Kk Ll

TROUBLEMAKERS COME AND GO BUT THEIR NAMES STICK WITH YOU FOREVER.

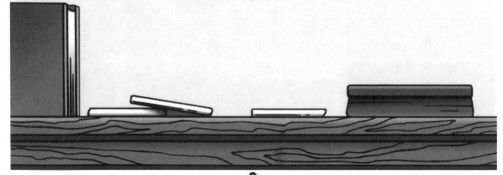

Aa Bb Cc Dd Ee Ff Gg Hh Ii Jj Kk Ll

YOU DISCOVER EVERYTHING YOU SAID IN THE TEACHER'S LOUNGE WAS SECRETLY RECORDED.

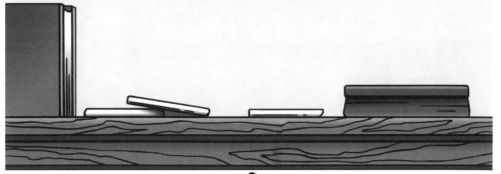

THE OFFICER DOUBLES YOUR SPEEDING TICKET WHEN HE DISCOVERS YOU WERE SPEEDING IN YOUR OWN SCHOOL ZONE.

THE PERSON YOU CUT OFF ON THE HIGHWAY TURNS OUT TO BE THE PARENT YOU'RE HAVING A CONFERENCE WITH THAT AFTERNOON.

YOU QUIT BEFORE YOU REALIZE YOUR WINNING LOTTERY NUMBERS WERE FOR THE WRONG DAY.

STRESS IS:
TRYING TO PRONOUNCE
THE WORDS AT THE
SPELLING BEE CONTEST.

Aa
Bb
Cc
Dd
Ee

WHEN YOU TASTE YOUR MORNING COFFEE, YOU REALIZE IT WAS LEFT OVER FROM YESTERDAY.

Zz
Yy
Xx
Ww
Vv
Uu
Tt
Ss

Ii Jj Kk Ll Mm Nn Oo Pp Qq Rr

14

Aa
Bb
Cc
Dd
Ee
Ff
Gg
Hh
Ii Jj Kk Ll Mm Nn Oo Pp Qq Rr

A STUDENT ASKS IF YOUR PMS CONDITION IS CONTAGIOUS.

Zz
Yy
Xx
Ww
Vv
Uu

BY OCTOBER, YOU'RE READY TO REQUEST A SUBSTITUTE TEACHER FOR THE REST OF THE SCHOOL YEAR.

THE THREE WORDS YOU DREAD MOST ARE, "BACK TO SCHOOL!"

YOUR TEACHING SKILLS ARE EVALUATED BY A PERSON WHO'S NEVER TAUGHT A CLASS IN HER LIFE.

THE PRINCIPAL SCHEDULES A PLANNING MEETING DURING YOUR SUMMER VACATION.

Aa Bb Cc Dd Ee Ff Gg Hh Ii Jj Kk Ll

YOU DIDN'T MAKE A LESSON PLAN BECAUSE YOU WERE JUST GOING TO SHOW A MOVIE ON THE SCHOOL'S TV. UNFORTUNATELY, ANOTHER TEACHER HAD THE SAME IDEA 5 MINUTES BEFORE YOU DID.

THE REAL REASON PARENTS WANT YEAR-ROUND SCHOOL IS SO THEY WON'T HAVE TO HIRE BABY-SITTERS IN THE SUMMER.

YOUR CLASS IS
SO BAD THE SUBSTITUTE
TEACHERS CALL IN SICK.

THE NOTE YOU TOOK UP IN CLASS IS A CRITIQUE OF YOUR OUTFIT.

STUDENTS TELL YOU THAT YOU HAVE CHALK IN YOUR HAIR. YOU TELL THEM IT'S GRAY.

STRESS IS:
USING UP ALL THE INK
IN YOUR RED PEN TO
CORRECT ONE PAPER!

Aa
Bb
Cc
Dd

SOMEHOW, YOUR SCHOOL PHOTOGRAPH IS WORSE THAN YOUR DRIVER'S LICENSE PICTURE.

Zz
Yy
Xx
Ww
Vv
Uu
Tt
Ss

Jj Kk Ll Mm Nn Oo Pp Qq Rr

26

Aa
Bb
Cc
Dd
Ee
Ff
Gg
Hh
Ii Jj Kk Ll Mm Nn Oo Pp Qq Rr

IT'S JUST A COINCIDENCE THAT YOU'RE SICK THE DAY OF A BIG SALE.

Zz
Yy
Xx
Ww
Vv
Uu

YOU WISH YOU HAD THE TEACHER'S EDITION TO THE "BOOK OF LIFE."

THE PRINCIPAL CHANGES THE MEETING TIME AND FORGETS TO TELL YOU.

STRESS IS:
DIRECTING THE
SCHOOL PLAY.

YOUR PRINCIPAL DECIDES TO HAVE A FIRE DRILL WHILE IT'S RAINING.

| Aa | Bb | Cc | Dd | Ee | Ff | Gg | Hh | Ii | Jj | Kk | Ll |

YOU KNOW IT'S BAD WHEN YOU USE THE WORD "LIKE" MORE TIMES IN A SENTENCE THAN YOUR STUDENTS.

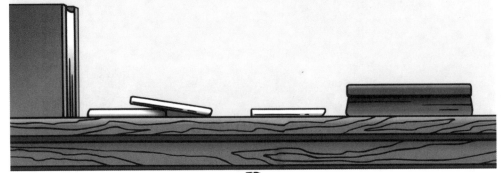

Aa Bb Cc Dd Ee Ff Gg Hh Ii Jj Kk Ll

HAVING AN UNSCHEDULED PARENT CONFERENCE IS NOT A GOOD WAY TO START THE WEEK.

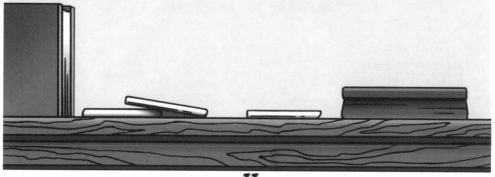

YOU NOTICE THE GOO ON THE WATER FOUNTAIN NOZZLE AFTER YOU'VE ALREADY TAKEN A DRINK.

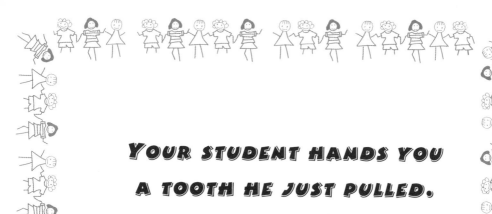

YOUR STUDENT HANDS YOU A TOOTH HE JUST PULLED.

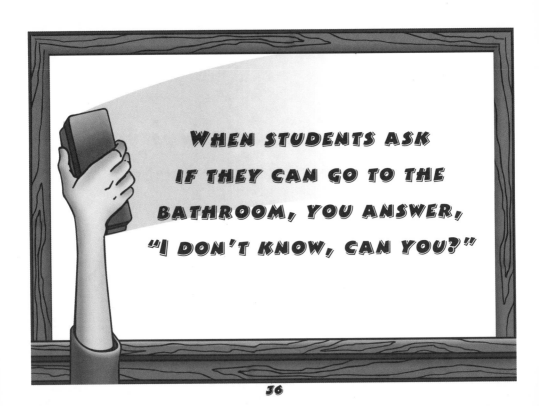

THE SCHOOL DISTRICT DISTRIBUTES TEACHER'S HOME PHONE NUMBERS TO PARENTS.

Aa Bb Cc Dd Ee

Zz Yy Xx Ww Vv Uu Tt Ss

Jj Kk Ll Mm Nn Oo Pp Qq Rr

Aa
Bb
Cc
Dd
Ee
Ff
Gg
Hh
Ii Jj Kk Ll Mm Nn Oo Pp Qq Rr

Zz
Yy
Xx
Ww
Vv
Uu

THE PRINCIPAL MENTIONS THAT YOU'RE THE ONLY PERSON KEEPING THE PARENT TEACHER ASSOCIATION FROM THEIR GOAL OF 100% PARTICIPATION.

WHY IS IT THAT STUDENTS STOP MINDING YOU ONCE THEIR PARENTS ARE AROUND?

STRESS IS:

TEACHING A COMPUTER CLASS TO STUDENTS WHO KNOW MORE ABOUT COMPUTERS THAN YOU DO.

YOU'RE THE LUCKY TEACHER RESPONSIBLE FOR CHECKING HAIR AND DRESS CODE VIOLATIONS.

YOU STORE TEACHING MATERIALS IN YOUR CAR BECAUSE THERE'S NO SPACE IN THE CLASSROOM.

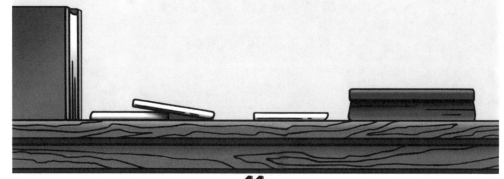

Aa Bb Cc Dd Ee Ff Gg Hh Ii Jj Kk Ll

YOU JUST FOUND

YESTERDAY'S URGENT

NOTE FROM

YOUR PRINCIPAL.

YOU HAVE TO SHARE YOUR LUNCH WITH THE BUGS IN YOUR DESK DRAWER.

46

A PRIVATE RESTROOM
BREAK IS A TRUE LUXURY.

YOU ACCIDENTALLY SET YOUR ALARM FOR P.M. INSTEAD OF A.M. ON THE FIRST DAY OF SCHOOL.

48

Aa
Bb
Cc
Dd

PARENTS DON'T UNDERSTAND THAT THE "NO PARKING" SIGNS IN THE SCHOOL PARKING LOT APPLY TO THEM.

Zz
Yy
Xx
Ww
Vv
Uu
Tt
Ss

Jj Kk Ll Mm Nn Oo Pp Qq Rr

YOU'VE BEEN INFORMED THAT A PET SNAKE IS LOST IN YOUR CLASSROOM.

Aa
Bb
Cc
Dd
Ee
Ff
Gg
Hh
Ii Jj Kk Ll Mm Nn Oo Pp Qq Rr

Zz
Yy
Xx
Ww
Vv
Uu
Tt
Ss

THERE'S A FOOD POISONING OUTBREAK THE DAY YOU EAT LUNCH IN THE SCHOOL CAFETERIA.

STRESS IS:
DISCOVERING THE
KEY TO THE TEST WAS
PHOTOCOPIED AND
DISTRIBUTED TO THE
ENTIRE CLASS.

WHY DO YOU HAVE TO GET YOUR MASTER'S DEGREE TO TEACH A KINDERGARTEN CLASS?

UPSET STOMACH:
CONDITION RESULTING
FROM READING
A PARENT'S NOTE
DURING LUNCH.

Aa Bb Cc Dd Ee Ff Gg Hh Ii Jj Kk Ll

YOUR WORST CLASS IS SELECTED TO PILOT A NEW LEARNING PROGRAM.

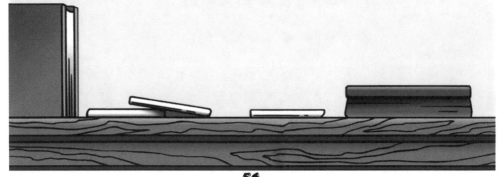

Aa Bb Cc Dd Ee Ff Gg Hh Ii Jj Kk Ll

**IF YOU WERE REIMBURSED
FOR TEACHING MATERIALS,
YOU'D BE RICH.**

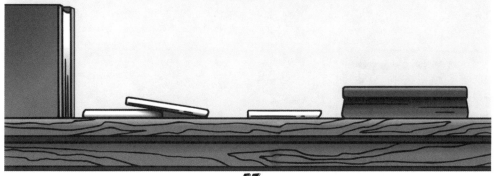

**YOU COULD WRITE
A ROMANCE NOVEL WITH THE
LOVE NOTES YOU'VE COLLECTED.**

BY THE TIME THE CROSSING GUARD GETS THE KIDS ACROSS THE STREET, THE SCHOOL ZONE HOURS ARE ALREADY OVER.

YOU DREAD ASSIGNING WRITTEN REPORTS BECAUSE YOU CAN'T READ HALF OF YOUR STUDENT'S HANDWRITING.

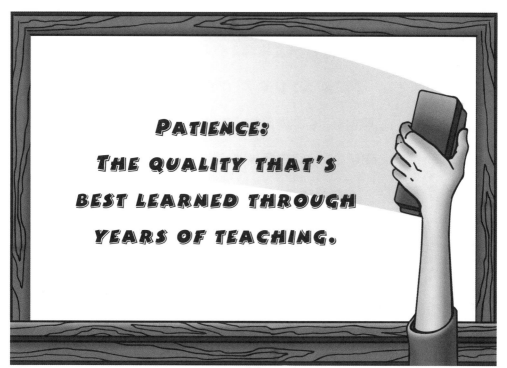

PATIENCE:
THE QUALITY THAT'S
BEST LEARNED THROUGH
YEARS OF TEACHING.

NUMEROLOGY:

THE STUDY OF WHY YOUR CLASS IS ALWAYS OVER-CROWDED WITH EXTRA STUDENTS.

Aa Bb Cc Dd

Zz Yy Xx Ww Vv Uu Tt Ss

Jj Kk Ll Mm Nn Oo Pp Qq Rr

THE PRINCIPAL GETS THE CREDIT FOR YOUR NEW TEACHING METHOD.

Aa Bb Cc Dd Ee Ff Gg Hh Ii Jj Kk Ll Mm Nn Oo Pp Qq Rr

Zz Yy Xx Ww Vv Uu

STRESS IS:
DELETING THE COMPUTER FILE
WITH YOUR CLASS GRADES.

YOU REMEMBER TO PASS OUT REPORT CARDS—AFTER THE STUDENTS HAVE ALREADY BEEN DISMISSED.

A SUBSTITUTE TEACHER COMPLAINS OF MENTAL ANGUISH AFTER TEACHING YOUR CLASS.

Your worst student returns as a student-teacher in your classroom.

THE VARICOSE VEINS IN YOUR LEGS SPELL OUT, "HELP!"

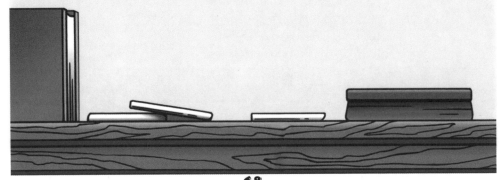

Aa Bb Cc Dd Ee Ff Gg Hh Ii Jj Kk Ll

YOU'VE NEVER REALLY PANICKED UNTIL YOU'VE LOST YOUR GRADE BOOK.

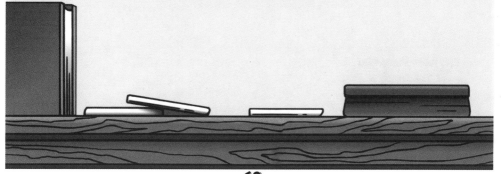

SOMETIMES IT WOULD BE EASIER TO SAY, "BECAUSE I SAID SO!"

**YOUR DESK IS SO FULL OF
THE TOYS YOU'VE CONFISCATED,
YOU DON'T HAVE ROOM FOR
YOUR OWN STUFF.**

A STUDENT POSTS YOUR SCHOOL GRADES ON THE INTERNET.

THE PRINCIPAL SCHEDULES MANDATORY MEETINGS DURING SPRING BREAK.

AUTOPHOBIA:
FEAR THAT YOUR
STUDENTS WILL
FIND OUT WHICH
CAR IS YOURS.

Aa Bb Cc Dd

Zz Yy Xx Ww Vv Uu Tt Ss

Ii Jj Kk Ll Mm Nn Oo Pp Qq Rr

74

NEVER MISS A STAFF MEETING OR THE WORK WILL BE ASSIGNED TO YOU.

Aa
Bb
Cc
Dd
Ee
Ff
Gg
Hh
Ii Jj Kk Ll Mm Nn Oo Pp Qq Rr

Zz
Yy
Xx
Ww
Vv
Uu

STRESS IS:
HAVING THE
SUPERINTENDENT'S SON
IN YOUR CLASS.

YOU WRITE MORE WITH CHALK THAN YOU DO WITH A PEN.

YOUR CLASS CONVINCED THE SUBSTITUTE TEACHER TO DISMISS THEM EARLY.

YOU RECEIVE A NOTE SAYING, "WHAT DO YOU MEAN YOU CAN'T READ MY SON'S HANDWRITING?" IN HANDWRITING THAT'S WORSE THAN THE CHILD'S.

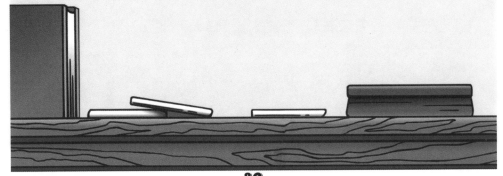

Aa Bb Cc Dd Ee Ff Gg Hh Ii Jj Kk Ll

YOUR IDEA OF CAPITAL PUNISHMENT
IS YEAR-ROUND SCHOOL.

Aa Bb Cc Dd Ee Ff Gg Hh Ii Jj Kk Ll

A PARENT WANTS TO KNOW WHY YOU MADE GRAMMATICAL CORRECTIONS TO THEIR NOTE.

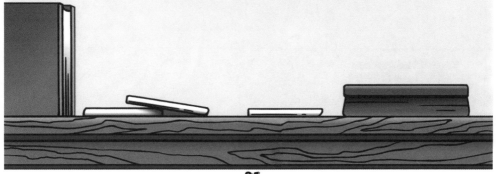

YOU SPELL THE PRINCIPAL'S NAME WRONG ON A RECOGNITION AWARD.

THE PERSON WHO SAID, "CHILDREN ARE THE FUTURE" NEVER MET YOUR CLASS!

YOU'RE MORE EXCITED ON THE LAST DAY OF SCHOOL THAN THE STUDENTS ARE!

STRESS IS:

DISCOVERING A NASTY PARENT NOTE WAS FORWARDED TO YOUR SUPERINTENDENT.

Aa
Bb
Cc
Dd

Zz
Yy
Xx
Ww
Vv
Uu
Tt
Ss

Jj Kk Ll Mm Nn Oo Pp Qq Rr

Aa
Bb
Cc
Dd
Ee
Ff
Gg
Hh
Ii Jj Kk Ll Mm Nn Oo Pp Qq Rr

Zz
Yy
Xx
Ww
Vv
Uu
Tt
Ss

THE CLASS HOLDS A CONTEST TO SEE WHO CAN SCRATCH THE CHALKBOARD THE LOUDEST.

RECIPE FOR DISASTER:
MIX OPEN HOUSE WITH
UNRULY STUDENTS.
BLEND IN IRATE PARENTS.

YOU HAVE RESPIRATORY PROBLEMS FROM ALL OF THE CHALK DUST YOU'VE INHALED.

A STUDENT WANTS TO KNOW IF HIS PARENT'S LAWSUIT AGAINST THE SCHOOL DISTRICT WILL AFFECT HIS GRADE.

YOU RECEIVE A MAKE-OVER GIFT FROM YOUR CLASS. WHAT ARE THEY TRYING TO SAY?

YOU SEE THE STUDENT YOU EXPELLED RUNNING FROM YOUR HOUSE.

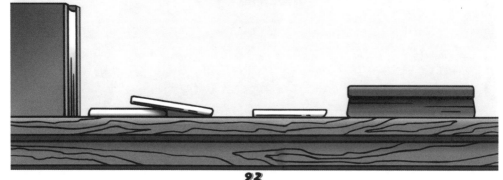

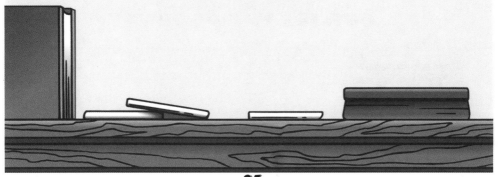

THE PARENT OF THE STUDENT YOU'RE DISCIPLINING IS STANDING OUTSIDE THE DOORWAY.

94

YOU HAVE A BLACK EYE FROM BREAKING UP A FIGHT (BETWEEN OTHER TEACHERS).

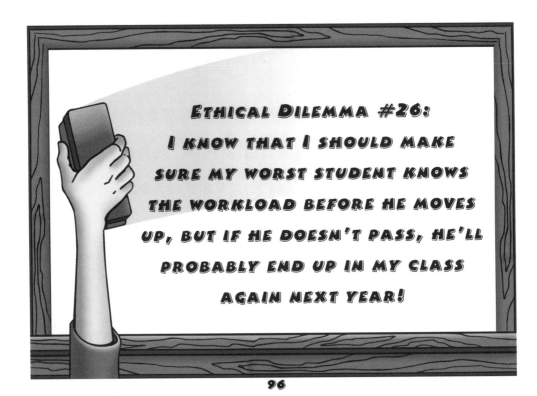

ETHICAL DILEMMA #26:
I KNOW THAT I SHOULD MAKE SURE MY WORST STUDENT KNOWS THE WORKLOAD BEFORE HE MOVES UP, BUT IF HE DOESN'T PASS, HE'LL PROBABLY END UP IN MY CLASS AGAIN NEXT YEAR!

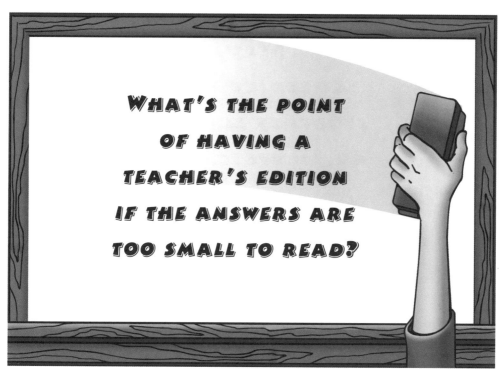

STRESS IS:
CATCHING YOUR
STUDENTS CHEATING
ON AN ETHICS TEST.

Aa Bb Cc Dd Ee

Zz Yy Xx Ww Vv Uu Tt Ss

Jj Kk Ll Mm Nn Oo Pp Qq Rr

HIDDEN WITHIN THE WORD "TEACHER" IS THE TRUE JOB DESCRIPTION: ACHE!

Aa
Bb
Cc
Dd
Ee
Ff
Gg
Hh
Ii Jj Kk Ll Mm Nn Oo Pp Qq Rr

Zz
Yy
Xx
Ww
Vv
Uu

YOU CREATED A "HOMEWORK EXCUSE HALL OF FAME."

THE PRINCIPAL "ENCOURAGES" YOU TO ATTEND ADDITIONAL TEACHER WORKSHOPS.

YOU LOOK FORWARD TO HAVING A CONVERSATION WITH AN ADULT.

WHEN ALL ELSE FAILS, GIVE A POP QUIZ.

FOR SOME MYSTERIOUS REASON, EVERY STUDENT MADE A 100 ON THE TEST...

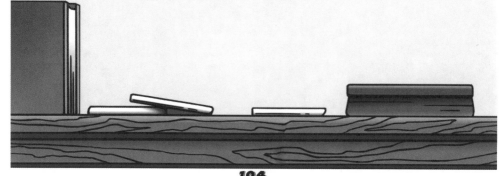

YOU KNOW YOU'VE BEEN TEACHING TOO LONG WHEN YOUR OWN CHILDREN ASK FOR PERMISSION TO GO TO THE BATHROOM!

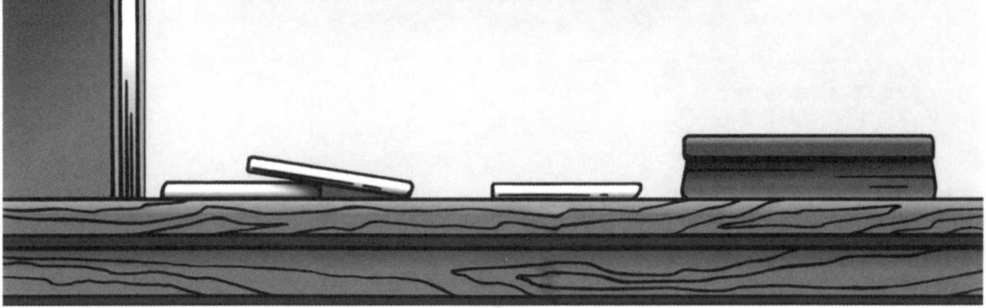

IT'S A BAD SIGN WHEN A PARENT'S SIGNATURE IS MISSPELLED ON A REPORT CARD.

STRESS IS:
LOSING YOUR VOICE ON THE DAY OF THE FIELD TRIP.

STUDENTS CREATE THEIR OWN SEATING CHART WHEN THERE'S A SUBSTITUTE TEACHER.

Cleaning up "accidents" in the classroom wasn't in the job description.

Aa
Bb
Cc
Dd
Ee

WHEN ALL ELSE FAILS,
REPEAT THE WORDS,
"JUNE, JULY
AND AUGUST!"

Zz
Yy
Xx
Ww
Vv
Uu
Tt
Ss

Ii Jj Kk Ll Mm Nn Oo Pp Qq Rr

Aa
Bb
Cc
Dd
Ee
Ff
Gg
Hh
Ii Jj Kk Ll Mm Nn Oo Pp Qq Rr

STRESS IS:
POURING A CUP OF
COFFEE ALL OVER THE
REPORT CARDS.

Zz
Yy
Xx
Ww
Vv
Uu

YOUR WORST STUDENT WEARS A "TEACHER'S PET" BUTTON.

**WHEN THE PRINCIPAL
SAYS PARTICIPATION
IS VOLUNTARY,
THINK AGAIN.**

THE PRINCIPAL JUST EXTENDED THE WORKDAY BY REQUIRING YOU TO TUTOR TWO HOURS AFTER THE BELL.

STRESS IS:
HAVING TO BORROW
LUNCH MONEY FROM STUDENTS.

IT'S FUNNY HOW THE
WORK LEFT FOR THE SUBSTITUTE
NEVER SEEMS TO GET DONE.

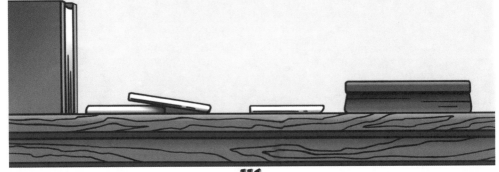

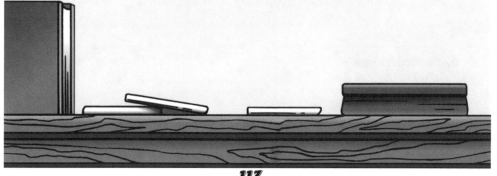

Aa Bb Cc Dd Ee Ff Gg Hh Ii Jj Kk Ll

YOUR STUDENTS
CHOOSE A ROACH
AS THE CLASS PET.

THE LESSON PLAN IS FOLLOWED ONLY WHEN YOU'RE ABSENT.

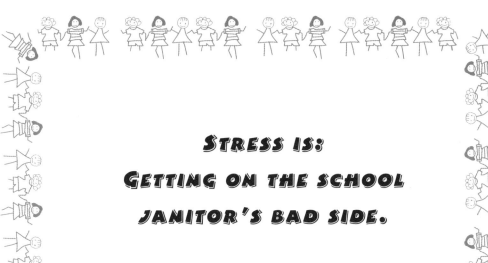

STRESS IS:
GETTING ON THE SCHOOL
JANITOR'S BAD SIDE.

119

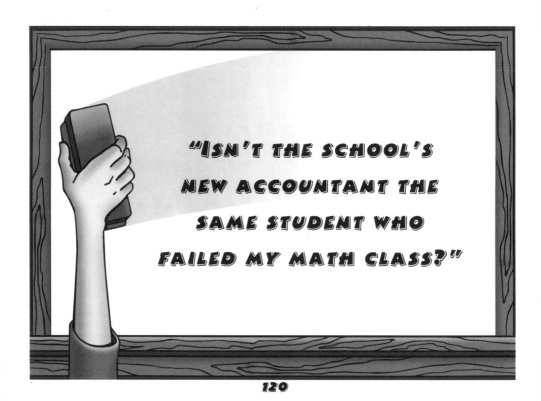

YOUR PRINCIPAL REVOKES YOUR PERSONAL DAYS OFF FOR MANDATORY TRAINING.

A STUDENT ASKS IF SHE'LL GET LEAD POISONING FROM EATING A #2 PENCIL.

STRESS IS... GRADING A COMPLETE SET OF TESTS USING THE WRONG ANSWER KEY.

You know it's going to be a rough year when no one makes an "A" in conduct.

STRESS IS:
DINGING THE PRINCIPAL'S
CAR DOOR IN THE
SCHOOL PARKING LOT.

IF YOU RUSH TO THE STORE IN YOUR WORST OUTFIT, YOU'LL ALWAYS RUN INTO A STUDENT.

YOU COULD START AN ELECTRONIC ZOO WITH ALL OF THE VIRTUAL PETS YOU'VE CONFISCATED.

STRESS IS:

**BEING SUMMONED FOR JURY DUTY
ON THE DAY OF FINAL EXAMS.**

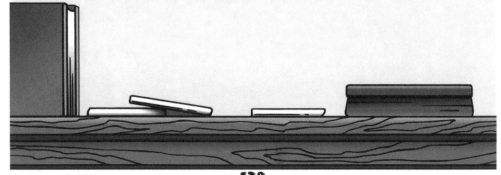

Aa Bb Cc Dd Ee Ff Gg Hh Ii Jj Kk Ll

A STUDENT ASKS YOU IF THE BOARD OF EDUCATION IS A PADDLE.

WHEN THE GOING GETS TOUGH CALL A SUB.

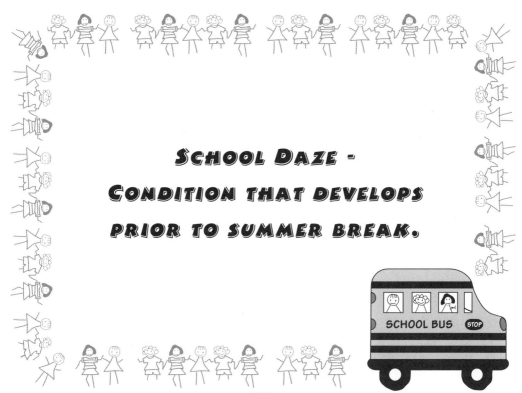

**SCHOOL DAZE -
CONDITION THAT DEVELOPS
PRIOR TO SUMMER BREAK.**

THE SCHOOL NURSE SHOWS UP AT YOUR CLASSROOM TO PERFORM A LICE CHECK.

A PARENT THINKS IT'S RUDE FOR YOU TO TEACH MANNERS IN CLASS.

Aa
Bb
Cc
Dd

CLASSROOM EXPERIENCE IS NOW EQUIVALENT TO "STREET SMARTS."

Zz
Yy
Xx
Ww
Vv
Uu
Tt
Ss

Jj Kk Ll Mm Nn Oo Pp Qq Rr

STRESS IS:

GETTING CAUGHT WITH YOUR OWN CAN OF SHAVING CREAM ON THE LAST DAY OF SCHOOL.

A STUDENT SAYS YOU NEED AN ATTITUDE ADJUSTMENT.

HALF WAY INTO THE FIELD TRIP, YOU REALIZE YOU FORGOT TO SEND OUT PERMISSION SLIPS.

STRESS IS:
LEADING THE
TEXTBOOK SELECTION
COMMITTEE.

WOULD'T IT BE GREAT TO BE A TEACHER AND MAKE A COACH'S SALARY?

Aa Bb Cc Dd Ee Ff Gg Hh Ii Jj Kk Ll

STUDENTS DISCOVER YOU WERE THE ONE WHO STARTED THE FOOD FIGHT.

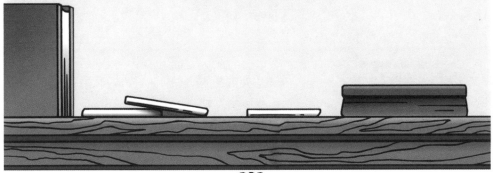

Aa Bb Cc Dd Ee Ff Gg Hh Ii Jj Kk Ll

YOUR STUDENTS HIDE ALL OF YOUR RED PENS.

AFTER COUNTING STUDENTS ON A FIELD TRIP, YOU COME UP ONE SHORT.

STRESS IS: FINDING OUT YOU DON'T QUALIFY FOR EARLY RETIREMENT.

THE JANITORS CLEAN YOUR CHALKBOARD AFTER YOU SPENT HOURS WRITING UP THE LESSON.

You're late to class the day after you teach a lesson on tardiness.

YOU KNOW YOU'RE A TEACHER IF YOU PUT CUTE LITTLE STICKERS ON YOUR SPOUSE'S WORK REPORTS.

Aa
Bb
Cc
Dd

Zz
Yy
Xx
Ww
Vv
Uu
Tt
Ss

Jj Kk Ll Mm Nn Oo Pp Qq Rr

HAVE YOU EVER FELT THE NEED TO REMIND YOUR FRIENDS TO BE COURTEOUS BY ASKING, "WHAT DO YOU SAY?" WHEN THEY FORGET TO SAY THANK YOU?

Aa Bb Cc Dd Ee Ff Gg Hh Ii Jj Kk Ll Mm Nn Oo Pp Qq Rr

Zz Yy Xx Ww Vv Uu

WHEN YOU KNOW THE ANSWER AT A TEACHER'S CONFERENCE, YOU SAY, "I KNOW! I KNOW! PICK ME!"

STRESS IS...
SEEING YOUR HOME PHONE NUMBER WRITTEN ON THE BATHROOM WALL.

NO MATTER HOW
MANY TIMES YOU
ANNOUNCE THE PAGE
NUMBER,
A STUDENT WILL
ALWAYS ASK AGAIN.

**YOUR STUDENTS'
BEST ACHIEVEMENT
TEST SCORES ARE THE
LOWEST IN THE SCHOOL.**

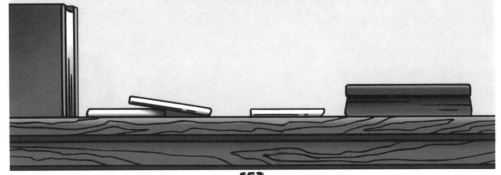

Aa Bb Cc Dd Ee Ff Gg Hh Ii Jj Kk Ll

STRESS IS: TRYING TO TEACH THE MOST DIFFICULT LESSON AFTER RECESS.

YOUR CAR IS OUT OF GAS THE DAY YOU'RE RUNNING LATE.

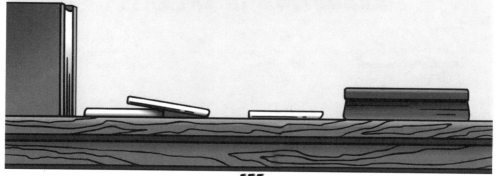

THE FOOTBALL TEAM GETS NEW UNIFORMS; YOU GET A REDUCTION IN SALARY.

154

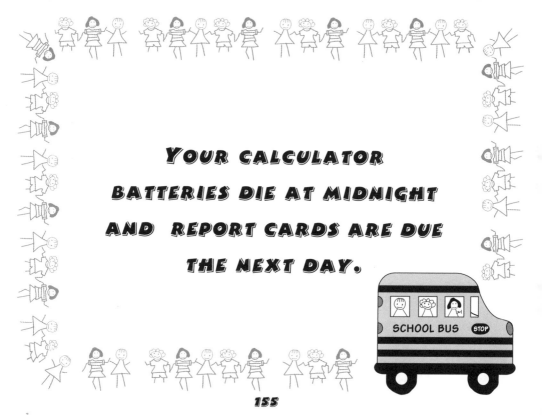

YOUR CALCULATOR BATTERIES DIE AT MIDNIGHT AND REPORT CARDS ARE DUE THE NEXT DAY.

SCHOOL BUS STOP

CORRECTING TYPOS BECOMES SECOND NATURE.

THE PRINCIPAL CATCHES YOU SKIPPING A WORKSHOP.

Aa
Bb
Cc
Dd

THE LEAD CHARACTER IN THE SCHOOL PLAY GETS CHICKEN POX.

Zz
Yy
Xx
Ww
Vv
Uu
Tt
Ss

Jj Kk Ll Mm Nn Oo Pp Qq Rr

Aa
Bb
Cc
Dd
Ee
Ff
Gg
Hh

IF YOUR LUNCH BREAK WERE ANY SHORTER, YOU'D HAVE TO GO ON A LIQUID DIET.

Zz
Yy
Xx
Ww
Vv
Uu

Ii Jj Kk Ll Mm Nn Oo Pp Qq Rr

STRESS IS:
FORGETTING TO CHANGE
THE CLOCK FOR
DAYLIGHT SAVINGS TIME.

THE WORDS YOU HATE TO HEAR THE MOST ARE, "MY MOM WANTS A PARENT-TEACHER CONFERENCE."

THE FIRST DAY OF SCHOOL IS ALWAYS THE LONGEST.

STRESS IS:
BEING THE ONLY TEACHER TO
FORGET THE PRINCIPAL'S BIRTHDAY.

Aa | Bb | Cc | Dd | Ee | Ff | Gg | Hh | Ii | Jj | Kk | Ll

PUNISHMENT IS HAVING TO USE THE STUDENT RESTROOM.

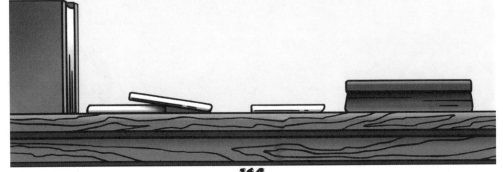

STRESS IS... THAT JUMBO BOX OF CRAYONS MELTED IN THE BACK SEAT OF YOUR CAR.

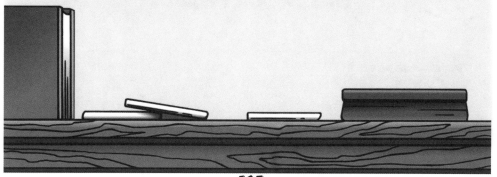

YOU'VE ALREADY SPENT YOUR RAISE IN THE SOFT DRINK MACHINE.